Contents

D1033312

Times have certainly changed since **OREO** cookie's delicious journey began a century ago, but those carefree **OREO** moments—TWIST, LICK, DUNK!—continue to bring out the playful kid inside each and every one of us. We've gathered some of the most inspired, fun, and altogether yummy recipes ever to include milk's favorite cookie.

For a celebration sensation, grab some pop sticks, because there's no party like a chocolate-frosted and bite-sized **OREO Party on a Stick**—and everyone's invited. You and your family will have as much fun dipping them as you will eating them—well, almost!

Winter holidays or summer feasts, is there ever a time when ice cream isn't in high demand? Part ice-cream sandwich, part fudge, the **OREO & Fudge Ice-Cream Cake** is made from a simple, no-bake recipe, so you can prepare it in advance. Bring a batch of luscious **Mini OREO Cheesecakes** to your next holiday party, anniversary, or reunion and watch the room fill with cheer. A smooth cream-cheese texture provides for a truly out-of-this-world experience. Oh, and don't forget the sprinkles!

Need to prepare something super easy for the next birthday party or after-school play date? You can let the whole family join in and assemble some cute and crunchy **OREO Frogs**. But make plenty, because these crowd-pleasing snacks have been known to leap right off the tray.

Whether a holiday feast or a graduation bash, sometimes an event calls for a true classic. The **Chocolate-Covered OREO Cookie Cake** has the stuff cake dreams are made of: two spongy devil's food cakes, cream cheese whipped filling and rich chocolate glaze—all in the shape of a giant **OREO** cookie!

When you make these delightful sweets with friends and loved ones, remember to relax, play, and celebrate the kid inside. As we honor 100 years of the delicious cookie that families love, let's raise a glass of milk to 100 more!

OREO Celebration Cookie Ball Pops

PREP: 20 MIN. PLUS REFRIGERATING | MAKES: 48 SERVINGS.

WHAT YOU NEED!

1 pkg. (8 oz.) cream cheese, softened

1 pkg. (15.5 oz.) OREO Cookies, finely crushed

8 oz. semi-sweet chocolate, melted

½ cup multi-colored sprinkles, divided

6 oz. white chocolate, melted

MAKE IT!

MIX cream cheese and cookie crumbs until blended.

SHAPE into 48 (1-inch) balls. Freeze 10 min. Insert lollipop stick into center of each ball. Dip 24 balls in semi-sweet chocolate; top with half the sprinkles. Place in single layer in shallow waxed paper-lined pan. Repeat with remaining balls, white chocolate and remaining sprinkles.

REFRIGERATE 1 hour or until firm.

HOW TO STORE: Store in tightly covered container in refrigerator.

OREO Birthday Cupcake Cake

PREP: 15 MIN. | MAKES: 24 SERVINGS.

WHAT YOU NEED!

- 1 pkg. (2-layer size) chocolate cake mix
- 24 OREO Cookies
- 1 chewy fruit snack roll
- 1 tub (12 oz.) frozen whipped topping, thawed
- 2 Tbsp. multi-colored sprinkles

MAKE IT!

HEAT oven to 350°F.

PREPARE cake batter and bake as directed on package for 24 cupcakes, placing 1 cookie in each paper-lined muffin cup before covering with batter. Cool completely.

MEANWHILE, cut fruit snack lengthwise into thirds. Wind each strip, in spiral fashion, around separate wooden spoon to form spiral. Place in shallow pan; freeze 10 min.

REMOVE cupcakes from paper liners just before serving. Arrange 12 cupcakes in circle on large plate; cover with 3 cups whipped topping and remaining cupcakes, top-sides down. Spoon remaining whipped topping onto center of cupcake stack; top with sprinkles. Carefully slide fruit snack spirals from spoons; use to garnish dessert. Serve immediately.

OREO Party on a Stick

PREP: 15 MIN. PLUS REFRIGERATING | MAKES: 12 SERVINGS.

WHAT YOU NEED!

12 OREO Cookies

6 oz. white chocolate, melted

1 tsp. canola oil

¼ cup multi-colored or chocolate sprinkles

MAKE IT!

INSERT wooden pop stick into filling in center of each cookie; place on waxed paper-covered rimmed baking sheet. Freeze 10 min.

MIX melted chocolate and oil until blended. Dip cookies, 1 at a time, in chocolate mixture, turning to evenly coat both sides of each. Return to baking sheet. Top with sprinkles.

REFRIGERATE 30 min. or until chocolate coating is firm.

SPECIAL EXTRA: Decorate cookies using sprinkles in the colors of your favorite sports team.

VARIATION: For variety, dip only 1 side of some of the cookie pops in melted chocolate before coating with sprinkles.

OREO PB & Banana Top Hat

PREP: 15 MIN. PLUS FREEZING | MAKES: 12 SERVINGS.

WHAT YOU NEED!

12 Peanut Butter Creme OREO Fudge Cremes

1 banana

4 oz. semi-sweet chocolate, melted, divided

1 Tbsp. multi-colored sprinkles

MAKE IT!

PLACE cookies in single layer in shallow parchment paper-lined pan. Cut banana into 12 slices.

POUR half the melted chocolate into small resealable plastic bag; set aside. Dip bottoms of banana slices, 1 at a time, in remaining melted chocolate; place on cookies. Snip small piece off bottom corner of chocolate-filled bag; drizzle chocolate over bananas. Top with sprinkles.

FREEZE 3 hours. Let stand at room temperature 5 min. before serving.

SHORTCUT: Prepare as directed, except do not place in freezer. Instead, refrigerate topped cookies 30 min. or until chocolate drizzle is firm.

Mini **OREO** Birthday "Cakes"

PREP: 30 MIN. PLUS REFRIGERATING | MAKES: 12 SERVINGS.

WHAT YOU NEED!

- 1 can (16 oz.) ready-to-spread white frosting, divided
- 24 OREO Cookies
- ¼ cup multi-colored sprinkles

MAKE IT!

PLACE wire rack over sheet of parchment paper. Measure ½ cup frosting; spoon ¼ tsp. onto top of each of 12 cookies. Cover with remaining cookies; press together gently to secure. Spread sides and tops of cookie stacks with remaining frosting (from ½ cup measure). Place on rack.

SPOON remaining frosting (from can) into microwaveable bowl. Microwave on HIGH 30 sec.; stir. Cool 2 min. Spoon ½ Tbsp. frosting over top of each cookie stack; repeat. Continue to spoon frosting over cookies until all frosting is used.

TOP with sprinkles. Refrigerate 1 hour or until frosting is firm.

OREO-Mini Ice Cream Tartlets

PREP: 20 MIN. PLUS FREEZING | MAKES: 12 SERVINGS.

WHAT YOU NEED!

- 24 OREO Cookies, finely crushed (about 2 cups)
- 2 Tbsp. butter or margarine, melted
- 3 cups BREYERS® OREO® Birthday Blast! Frozen Dairy Dessert*, softened
- ¼ cup thawed frozen whipped topping
- 12 Mini OREO Bite Size Cookies

MAKE IT!

MIX cookie crumbs and butter.

SCOOP ¼ cup ice cream into each of 12 paper-lined muffin cups. Top each with 1½ Tbsp. crumb mixture; press into ice cream to secure. Freeze 3 hours or until firm.

REMOVE tarts from muffin pan; discard paper liners. Place tarts, crumb-sides down, on dessert plates; top with whipped topping and mini cookies.

SUBSTITUTE: *BREYERS® OREO® Birthday Blast! Frozen Dairy Dessert is a limited edition ice cream. Substitute using BREYERS® OREO® Cookies & Cream Frozen Dairy Dessert.

BREYERS® is a registered trademark of the Unilever Group of Companies. ©Unilever.

OREO Heads Or Tails "The Bombe"

PREP: 30 MIN. PLUS FREEZING | MAKES: 12 SERVINGS.

WHAT YOU NEED!

1 pkg. (15.25 oz.) DOUBLE STUF OREO Heads Or Tails

1 pkg. (3.9 oz.) chocolate instant pudding

1 pkg. (3.3 oz.) white chocolate flavor instant pudding

2 cups cold milk, divided

2 cups thawed frozen whipped topping, divided

MAKE IT!

LINE 1½-qt. freezerproof bowl with plastic wrap, allowing 3-inch piece to extend over top of bowl. Arrange 22 cookies alternately around inside of bowl, cutting to make even with edge of bowl if necessary. Chop remaining cookies.

BEAT each flavor dry pudding mix and 1 cup milk in separate bowl with whisk 2 min. Stir 1 cup whipped topping into pudding in each bowl until blended. Layer puddings in cookie-lined bowl, sprinkling ½ of the chopped cookies between layers. Top with remaining cookies; cover.

FREEZE 4 hours or until firm. Remove from freezer 20 min. before serving. Let stand at room temperature to soften slightly. Unmold dessert onto plate. Remove plastic wrap.

MAKE AHEAD: Dessert can be frozen, tightly wrapped in foil, up to 1 week before serving.

OREO Crispy Treat Pops

PREP: 10 MIN. PLUS COOLING | MAKES: 18 SERVINGS.

WHAT YOU NEED!

- 3 Tbsp. butter or margarine
- 1 pkg. (10 oz.) marshmallows
- 5 cups crisp rice cereal
- 16 OREO Cookies, coarsely chopped (about 2 cups)
- 4 oz. semi-sweet chocolate, melted
- ¼ cup multi-colored sprinkles

MAKE IT!

MICROWAVE butter in large microwaveable bowl on HIGH 45 sec. or until melted. Add marshmallows; toss to coat. Microwave 1½ min. or until marshmallows are completely melted and mixture is well blended, stirring after 45 sec.

ADD cereal and chopped cookies; mix well. Press onto bottom of 9-inch square pan sprayed with cooking spray. Cool completely.

CUT into 18 bars. Insert lollipop stick into one short end of each. Dip ends in chocolate; top with sprinkles. Refrigerate 10 min. or until chocolate is firm.

OREO Candy Cane Bark

PREP: 10 MIN. PLUS REFRIGERATING | MAKES: 1½ LB. OR 18 SERVINGS.

WHAT YOU NEED!

18 oz. white chocolate

15 OREO Cookies, coarsely chopped (about 2 cups)

3 candy canes, crushed (about ¼ cup)

MAKE IT!

COVER large baking sheet with foil; set aside. Microwave chocolate in large microwaveable bowl on HIGH 2 min. or until almost melted, stirring every 30 sec. Stir until chocolate is completely melted. Stir in chopped cookies.

SPREAD immediately onto prepared baking sheet. Sprinkle with crushed candy canes; press candy lightly into chocolate with back of spoon.

REFRIGERATE 4 hours or until firm. Break into pieces. Store in tightly covered container in refrigerator.

CRUSHING CANDY CANES:

Crushing candy canes can be a messy task. To keep the crushed candy contained, place candy canes in a resealable plastic bag and squeeze air from bag; seal. Use a rolling pin or meat mallet to crush the candy into small pieces.

OREO-Apple Snack Stacks

PREP: 15 MIN. | MAKES: 8 SERVINGS.

WHAT YOU NEED!

- 1 pkg. (8 oz.) cream cheese, softened
- 2 Tbsp. honey
- ½ tsp. zest and 2 Tbsp. juice from 1 orange, divided
- 6 OREO Cookies, chopped
- 4 small apples (1 lb.)
- 4 pretzel sticks
- 8 worm-shaped chewy fruit snacks

MAKE IT!

MIX cream cheese, honey and zest in medium bowl until well blended. Stir in chopped cookies. Core apples. Cut each crosswise into 4 rings; brush cut sides with orange juice. Discard any remaining juice.

PAT apple slices dry with paper towels; spread with cream cheese mixture. Restack slices for each apple. Insert pretzel into top of each for the stem.

GARNISH with fruit snacks. Cut horizontally in half to serve.

MAKE AHEAD: Snacks can be made ahead of time. Prepare as directed; wrap with plastic wrap. Refrigerate until ready to serve.

Cherry-Vanilla Ice Cream Pie

PREP: 20 MIN. PLUS FREEZING | MAKES: 10 SERVINGS.

WHAT YOU NEED!

18 OREO Cookies, finely crushed (about 1½ cups)

3 Tbsp. butter or margarine, melted

3 cups vanilla ice cream, softened

1 can (21 oz.) cherry pie filling, divided

1 Tbsp. chocolate syrup

MAKE IT!

COMBINE cookie crumbs and butter; press onto bottom and up side of 9-inch pie plate sprayed with cooking spray. Refrigerate until ready to use.

MIX ice cream and 1½ cups pie filling; spoon into crust. Freeze 4 hours or until firm.

DRIZZLE chocolate syrup over pie. Serve topped with remaining cherry pie filling.

SUBSTITUTE: Prepare using a chocolate syrup that hardens to form a "shell" when drizzled over the pie.

OREO No-Bake Cheesecake

PREP: 15 MIN. PLUS REFRIGERATING | MAKES: 16 SERVINGS, 1 PIECE EACH.

WHAT YOU NEED!

1 pkg. (16.6 oz.) OREO
Cookies, divided

¼ cup butter, melted

4 pkg. (8 oz. each) cream
cheese, softened

½ cup sugar

1 tsp. vanilla

1 tub (8 oz.) frozen whipped
topping, thawed

MAKE IT!

LINE 13×9-inch pan with foil, with
ends of foil extending over sides of pan.
Coarsely chop 15 of the cookies; set
aside. Finely crush remaining cookies; mix
with butter. Press firmly onto bottom of
prepared pan. Refrigerate while preparing
filling.

BEAT cream cheese, sugar and vanilla in
large bowl with electric mixer on medium
speed until well blended. Gently stir in
whipped topping and chopped cookies.
Spoon over crust; cover.

REFRIGERATE 4 hours or until
firm. Store leftover cheesecake in
refrigerator.

VARIATION: Prepare as
directed, using 1 pkg.
(1 lb. 2 oz.) Golden **OREO**
Cookies or 1 pkg. (1 lb.
1 oz.) **OREO** Cool Mint
Creme Cookies.

White Chocolate-**OREO** Fudge

PREP: 30 MIN. | MAKES: ABOUT 4 LB. OR 48 SERVINGS.

WHAT YOU NEED!

30 OREO Cookies, divided

3 cups sugar

¾ cup butter or margarine

1 can (5 oz.) evaporated milk (about ⅔ cup)

12 oz. white chocolate

1 jar (7 oz.) marshmallow creme

1 tsp. vanilla

MAKE IT!

CHOP 10 cookies coarsely; finely crush remaining cookies. Line 9-inch square pan with foil, with ends of foil extending over sides. Spray lightly with cooking spray; press half the finely crushed cookies onto bottom of pan.

BRING sugar, butter and evaporated milk to full rolling boil in 3-qt. saucepan on medium heat, stirring constantly. Cook 4 min. or until candy thermometer reaches 234°F, stirring constantly. Remove from heat.

ADD white chocolate and marshmallow creme; stir until melted. Stir in vanilla and coarsely chopped cookies; carefully spread over cookies in pan. Top with remaining finely crushed cookies; press into fudge with back of spoon. Cool completely. Use foil handles to lift fudge from pan before cutting into squares.

OREO & Fudge Ice Cream Cake

WHAT YOU NEED!

½ cup hot fudge ice cream topping, warmed

1 tub (8 oz.) frozen whipped topping, thawed, divided

1 pkg. (3.9 oz.) chocolate instant pudding

16 OREO Cookies, chopped, divided

12 vanilla ice cream sandwiches

MAKE IT!

POUR fudge topping into medium bowl. Whisk in 1 cup whipped topping. Add dry pudding mix; stir 2 min. Stir in 1 cup chopped cookies.

ARRANGE 4 ice cream sandwiches, side-by-side, on 24-inch-long piece of foil; top with half the whipped topping mixture. Repeat layers. Top with remaining sandwiches. Frost top and sides with remaining whipped topping; press remaining chopped cookies into whipped topping on top and sides of cake. Bring up foil sides; double fold top and ends to loosely seal packet.

FREEZE 4 hours.

NOTE: The consistency of fudge topping can vary depending on what brand you purchase. If your fudge topping mixture is too thick to spread easily, stir in up to ¼ cup milk.

Cookies & Cream Freeze

PREP: 30 MIN. PLUS FREEZING | MAKES: 12 SERVINGS, 1 PIECE EACH.

WHAT YOU NEED!

4 oz. semi-sweet chocolate

14 OREO Cookies, divided

1 pkg. (8 oz.) cream cheese, softened

¼ cup sugar

½ tsp. vanilla

1 tub (8 oz.) frozen whipped topping, thawed

MAKE IT!

MELT chocolate as directed on package; set aside until ready to use. Line 8½×4½-inch loaf pan with foil, with ends of foil extending over sides of pan. Arrange 8 of the cookies evenly on bottom of pan. Crumble remaining 6 cookies; set aside.

BEAT cream cheese, sugar and vanilla in medium bowl with electric mixer until well blended. Stir in whipped topping. Remove about 1½ cups of the cream cheese mixture; place in medium bowl. Stir in melted chocolate.

SPREAD remaining cream cheese mixture over cookies in pan; sprinkle with crumbled cookies. Gently press cookies into cream cheese mixture with back of spoon; top with chocolate mixture. Cover. Freeze 3 hours or until firm. Remove from freezer about 15 min. before serving; invert onto serving plate. Peel off foil; let stand at room temperature to soften slightly before cutting to serve.

SPECIAL EXTRA: Drizzle serving plates with additional melted semi-sweet chocolate for a spectacular, yet simple, dessert presentation.

Frozen **OREO** Fudge-Pop Squares

PREP: 15 MIN. PLUS FREEZING | MAKES: 16 SERVINGS, 1 SQUARE EACH.

WHAT YOU NEED!

5 oz. semi-sweet chocolate

18 OREO Cookies, crushed

3 Tbsp. butter or margarine, melted

2 tubs (8 oz. each) cream cheese spread

1 can (14 oz.) sweetened condensed milk

1 cup thawed frozen whipped topping

MAKE IT!

LINE 9-inch square pan with foil, with ends of foil extending over sides. Melt 4 oz. chocolate as directed on package; set aside. Mix cookie crumbs and butter; press onto bottom of prepared pan.

BEAT cream cheese spread in large bowl with mixer until creamy. Gradually beat in sweetened condensed milk. Blend in chocolate. Whisk in whipped topping. Spoon over crust. Freeze 6 hours. Meanwhile, make curls from remaining chocolate.

REMOVE dessert from freezer 15 min. before serving. Top with chocolate curls. Use foil handles to lift dessert from pan.

HOW TO MAKE CHOCOLATE CURLS: Warm 1 oz. chocolate by microwaving it, unwrapped, on HIGH for a few sec., or just until you can smudge the chocolate with your thumb. Hold the chocolate steadily and draw a peeler slowly over flat bottom, allowing a thin layer of chocolate to curl as it's peeled off to make long, delicate curls. Use the same technique along the narrow side of the chocolate to make short curls.

OREO S'mores Brownies

PREP: 15 MIN. PLUS BAKING | MAKES: 24 SERVINGS.

WHAT YOU NEED!

7½ HONEY MAID Honey Grahams, broken in half

1 pkg. (19 to 21 oz.) brownie mix (13×9-inch pan size)

4 oz. white chocolate, chopped

1 cup miniature marshmallows

8 OREO Cookies, chopped, divided

MAKE IT!

HEAT oven to 350°F.

LINE 13×9-inch pan with foil, with ends of foil extending over sides; spray with cooking spray. Arrange graham squares in single layer on bottom of pan, overlapping slightly if necessary.

PREPARE brownie batter as directed on package; stir in chopped chocolate, marshmallows and ¾ cup chopped cookies. Spread over grahams; sprinkle with remaining cookies.

BAKE 27 to 30 min. or until toothpick inserted 1 inch from edge of pan comes out clean. Cool completely. Use foil handles to lift brownie from pan before cutting to serve.

SPECIAL EXTRA: Add ½ cup chopped walnuts or pecans to batter before pouring into prepared pan.

Double-Dipped Strawberries

PREP: 10 MIN. | MAKES: 10 SERVINGS, 1 DIPPED STRAWBERRY EACH.

WHAT YOU NEED!

10 fresh strawberries (about 1 pt.), washed, well dried

4 oz. semi-sweet chocolate, melted

8 OREO Cookies, coarsely crushed (about 1 cup crumbs)

MAKE IT!

DIP strawberries in melted chocolate; roll in crumbs.

PLACE on waxed paper-covered baking sheet; let stand until chocolate is firm.

SUBSTITUTE: Prepare using white chocolate.

Double-Chocolate **OREO** Fudge

PREP: 30 MIN. | MAKES: 6¼ LB. OR 72 SERVINGS, 1 PIECE EACH.

WHAT YOU NEED!

6 cups sugar, divided

1½ cups butter or margarine, divided

2 small cans (5 oz. each) evaporated milk (about ⅔ cup each)

12 oz. semi-sweet chocolate

2 jars (7 oz. each) marshmallow creme, divided

1 cup chopped macadamias

2 tsp. vanilla, divided

12 oz. white chocolate

8 OREO Cookies, chopped

MAKE IT!

LINE 13×9-inch pan with foil, with ends of foil extending over sides of pan. Place 3 cups sugar, ¾ cup butter and 1 can evaporated milk in heavy 3-qt. saucepan. Bring to full rolling boil on medium heat, stirring constantly. Boil 4 min. or until candy thermometer reaches 234°F, stirring constantly to prevent scorching. Remove from heat.

ADD semi-sweet chocolate and 1 jar marshmallow creme; stir until melted. Add macadamias and 1 tsp. vanilla; mix well. Pour into prepared pan; spread to evenly cover bottom of pan. Set aside.

PLACE remaining 3 cups sugar, remaining ¾ cup butter and remaining can of evaporated milk in same saucepan. Bring to full rolling boil on medium heat, stirring constantly. Boil 4 min. or until candy thermometer reaches 234°F, stirring constantly. Remove from heat.

ADD white chocolate and remaining jar of marshmallow creme; stir until melted. Add chopped cookies and remaining 1 tsp. vanilla; mix well. Pour over semi-sweet chocolate layer in pan; spread to evenly cover. Cool at room temperature at least 4 hours before cutting into small pieces to serve. Store in tightly covered container at room temperature.

Mini **OREO** Cheesecakes

PREP: 15 MIN. PLUS BAKING AND REFRIGERATING | MAKES: 2 DOZ. OR 24 SERVINGS.

WHAT YOU NEED!

44 OREO Cookies, divided

3 pkg. (8 oz. each) cream cheese, softened

¾ cup sugar

¾ cup sour cream

1 tsp. vanilla

3 eggs

2 oz. white chocolate, melted

½ cup colored sprinkles

1½ cups thawed frozen whipped topping

MAKE IT!

HEAT oven to 325°F.

PLACE 1 cookie in each of 24 foil- or paper-lined muffin pan cups. Chop 8 of the remaining cookies; set aside.

BEAT cream cheese and sugar with mixer until blended. Add sour cream and vanilla; mix well. Add eggs, 1 at a time, beating after each just until blended. Gently stir in chopped cookies. Spoon into baking cups.

BAKE 18 to 20 min. or until centers are set. Cool completely. Refrigerate 3 hours or until chilled. Meanwhile, cut remaining cookies in half. Dip cookie halves halfway in melted chocolate. Place on waxed paper-covered baking sheet; top with sprinkles. Let stand 15 min. or until chocolate is firm.

TOP each cheesecake with dollop of whipped topping and cookie half just before serving.

MAKE AHEAD: Cheesecakes can be stored in refrigerator up to 3 days, or frozen up to 1 month, before topping with whipped topping and cookie half just before serving. If freezing cheesecakes, thaw overnight in refrigerator before garnishing.

Cookie "Fun-Due"

PREP: 10 MIN. | **MAKES: 1¾ CUPS OR 14 SERVINGS, 2 TBSP. DIP AND 3 COOKIES EACH.**

WHAT YOU NEED!

8 oz. semi-sweet chocolate

1 cup whipping cream

OREO Cookies

MAKE IT!

MICROWAVE chocolate and whipping cream in large microwaveable bowl on HIGH 2 min. or until chocolate is completely melted and mixture is well blended, stirring after each min.

SERVE warm with cookies for dipping.

SPECIAL EXTRA: Serve with additional dippers, such as vanilla wafers, chocolate chip cookies, graham crackers, marshmallows, strawberries, banana chunks and apple slices.

OREO Cheesecake Bites

PREP: 20 MIN. PLUS BAKING AND REFRIGERATING | MAKES: 36 SERVINGS, 1 BAR EACH.

WHAT YOU NEED!

36 OREO Cookies, divided

½ cup butter or margarine, divided

4 pkg. (8 oz. each) cream cheese, softened

1 cup sugar

1 tsp. vanilla

1 cup sour cream

4 eggs

4 oz. semi-sweet chocolate

MAKE IT!

HEAT oven to 325°F.

LINE 13×9-inch baking pan with foil. Finely crush 24 cookies. Melt ¼ cup butter; mix with crumbs. Press onto bottom of pan.

BEAT cream cheese, sugar and vanilla with mixer until blended. Add sour cream; mix well. Add eggs, 1 at a time, beating just until blended after each addition. Chop remaining cookies. Gently stir into batter; pour over crust.

BAKE 45 min. or until center is almost set. Cool. Meanwhile, place chocolate and remaining ¼ cup butter in microwaveable bowl. Microwave on HIGH 1 min. Stir until smooth. Cool slightly; pour over cheesecake. Spread to cover top of cheesecake. Refrigerate at least 4 hours. Remove cheesecake from pan before cutting to serve.

NOTE: When lining pan with foil, extend ends of foil over sides of pan to use as handles when removing cheesecake from pan.

Peppermint-**OREO**.Cookie Balls

PREP: 20 MIN. PLUS REFRIGERATING | MAKES: 48 SERVINGS.

WHAT YOU NEED!

6 candy canes, finely chopped (about ⅓ cup), divided

1 pkg. (8 oz.) cream cheese, softened

1 pkg. (15.5 oz.) OREO Cookies, finely crushed

16 oz. semi-sweet chocolate, melted

MAKE IT!

RESERVE 1 Tbsp. chopped candy. Mix remaining candy with cream cheese and cookie crumbs until well blended.

SHAPE into 48 (1-inch) balls. Freeze 10 min. Dip balls in melted chocolate; place in single layer in shallow waxed paper-lined pan. Sprinkle with reserved candy.

REFRIGERATE 1 hour or until firm.

HOW TO STORE:
Store in tightly covered container in refrigerator.

OREO Chocolate-Raspberry Truffle Cups

PREP: 30 MIN. PLUS REFRIGERATING | MAKES: 2 DOZ. OR 24 SERVINGS.

WHAT YOU NEED!

- ¼ cup butter or margarine, divided
- 12 OREO Cookies, finely crushed (about 1 cup)
- 2 Tbsp. raspberry jam
- 6 oz. white chocolate
- ½ cup whipping cream, divided
- 6 oz. semi-sweet chocolate
- 2 Tbsp. white or multi-colored sprinkles

MAKE IT!

MELT 2 Tbsp. butter; mix with cookie crumbs. Press onto bottoms of 24 miniature paper-lined muffin cups. Add ¼ tsp. jam to each. Refrigerate until ready to use.

MICROWAVE white chocolate, ¼ cup cream and 1 Tbsp. of the remaining butter in microwaveable bowl on HIGH 1 min.; stir until chocolate is melted and mixture is well blended. Spoon over jam. Freeze 10 min.

MEANWHILE, melt semi-sweet chocolate with remaining cream and butter as directed for white chocolate. Spoon over white chocolate layer; top with sprinkles. Refrigerate 1 to 2 hours or until firm.

SUBSTITUTE: For variety, substitute marshmallow creme, peanut butter, caramel sauce or a different flavor of jam for the raspberry jam in the recipe.

Martians-Ate-My-**OREO** Cupcakes

PREP: 20 MIN. PLUS BAKING AND COOLING | MAKES: 2 DOZ. OR 24 SERVINGS.

WHAT YOU NEED!

- 1 pkg. (2-layer size) chocolate cake mix
- 1 pkg. (8 oz.) cream cheese, softened
- 1 egg
- 2 Tbsp. sugar
- 54 Mini OREO Cookies, divided
- 2 or 3 drops green food coloring
- 2 cups thawed frozen whipped topping
- 4 OREO Cookies
- ¼ cup miniature marshmallows
- 4 marshmallows, cut in half
- 2 pieces string licorice
- 1 Tbsp. assorted round candies

MAKE IT!

HEAT oven to 350°F.

PREPARE cake batter as directed on package. Mix cream cheese, egg and sugar until well blended. Spoon half the cake batter into 24 paper-lined muffin cups. Top each with about 2 tsp. cream cheese mixture and 1 mini cookie; cover with remaining batter.

BAKE 19 to 22 min. or until toothpick inserted in centers comes out clean. Cool 5 min.; remove from pans to wire racks. Cool completely.

STIR green food coloring into whipped topping spread onto cupcakes. Split remaining mini and regular-size cookies, leaving all the filling on half of each cookie. Use with remaining ingredients to decorate cupcakes to resemble martians as shown in photo.

OREO Turkey

WHAT YOU NEED!

- 6 OREO Cookies
- 1 oz. semi-sweet chocolate, melted
- 30 pieces candy corn
- 6 chocolate malted milk balls
- 6 cinnamon red hot candies

MAKE IT!

SEPARATE each cookie, leaving all the cream filling on 1 half of each. Set filling-topped halves aside.

USE small amount of melted chocolate to attach 5 candy corn pieces, pointed-sides down, to each plain cookie half for the turkey's tail. Refrigerate 5 min. or until chocolate is firm.

ATTACH malted milk ball to center of each filling-topped cookie half with melted chocolate for the turkey's body. Use dot of melted chocolate to attach cinnamon candy to each body for the head.

ATTACH turkey tails to bodies with remaining melted chocolate. Refrigerate until firm.

HOW TO EASILY SEPARATE COOKIES:
Refrigerate cookies for 15 min. before carefully twisting top from bottom so that the cream remains entirely on 1 half of the cookie. Use a knife to smooth filling if necessary.

OREO Cookies & Creme Pudding Pops

PREP: 10 MIN. PLUS FREEZING | MAKES: 10 SERVINGS.

WHAT YOU NEED!

1 pkg. (3.4 oz.) vanilla flavor instant pudding

2 cups cold milk

12 OREO Cookies, divided

½ cup thawed frozen whipped topping

MAKE IT!

BEAT dry pudding mix and milk in medium bowl with whisk 2 min.

CHOP 6 cookies; crush remaining cookies. Spoon half the crushed cookies onto bottoms of 10 (3-oz.) paper or plastic cups.

ADD chopped cookies and whipped topping to pudding; stir just until blended.

SPOON pudding mixture into cups; top with remaining crushed cookies. Insert wooden pop stick or plastic spoon into each for handle. Freeze 5 hours or until firm.

HOW TO REMOVE FROZEN POPS FROM CUPS: Hold frozen cups with hands on sides of cups to warm pops slightly before removing from cups. To remove pops, press firmly onto bottom of cup to release pop. Do not twist or pull pop stick.

Dirt Cups

PREP: 15 MIN. PLUS REFRIGERATING | MAKES: 10 SERVINGS.

WHAT YOU NEED!

- 1 pkg. (3.9 oz.) chocolate instant pudding
- 2 cups cold milk
- 1 tub (8 oz.) frozen whipped topping, thawed
- 15 OREO Cookies, finely crushed (about 1¼ cups), divided
- 10 worm-shaped chewy fruit snacks

MAKE IT!

BEAT dry pudding mix and milk in large bowl with whisk 2 min. Let stand 5 min. Stir in whipped topping and ½ cup cookie crumbs.

SPOON into 10 (6- to 7-oz.) plastic or paper cups; top with remaining cookie crumbs.

REFRIGERATE 1 hour. Top with fruit snacks just before serving.

OREO Baseball Dessert

PREP: 15 MIN. PLUS REFRIGERATING | MAKES: 10 SERVINGS.

WHAT YOU NEED!

1 pkg. (3.9 oz.) chocolate instant pudding

2 cups cold milk

35 OREO Cookies, divided

1½ cups thawed frozen whipped topping

1 piece red string licorice (36 inches)

MAKE IT!

BEAT dry pudding mix and milk with whisk 2 min. Let stand 5 min. or until thickened.

LINE 8-inch round pan with plastic wrap. Arrange 14 cookies on bottom of pan, cutting to fit if necessary; cover with 1 cup pudding. Repeat layers. Cover with plastic wrap. Refrigerate 24 hours.

UNCOVER dessert. Invert onto serving plate; remove plastic wrap. Frost dessert with whipped topping. Cut remaining cookies in half; arrange around edge of dessert. Cut licorice into 2 (8-inch) pieces and 20 (1-inch) pieces. Use licorice to decorate top of dessert to resemble a baseball.

HOW TO EASILY CUT COOKIES IN HALF:

Refrigerate **OREO** Cookies first for about 15 min. Then, use a serrated knife to cut in half.

OREO Frogs

PREP: 20 MIN. | MAKES: 6 SERVINGS.

WHAT YOU NEED!

- 2 oz. semi-sweet chocolate
- 2 Tbsp. butter or margarine
- 12 OREO Cookies
- ¼ cup marshmallow creme
- 24 miniature pretzel twists
- 24 candy-coated chocolate pieces

MAKE IT!

MICROWAVE chocolate and butter in microwaveable bowl on HIGH 1 min. or until chocolate is completely melted and mixture is well blended, stirring every 30 sec.

SPREAD bottom of each cookie with 1 tsp. marshmallow creme, then dip bottom in melted chocolate. Immediately press 2 pretzel twists into chocolate for each frog's legs, with wide part of each pretzel facing outward. Place, pretzel-sides down, on waxed paper-covered baking sheet.

USE remaining melted chocolate to attach candies to tops of cookies for frog's eyes. Let stand until chocolate is firm.

OREO Milk Shake

PREP: 10 MIN. | MAKES: 4 SERVINGS, ABOUT 1 CUP EACH.

WHAT YOU NEED!

4 tsp. chocolate syrup

8 OREO Cookies, divided

1½ cups milk

2 cups vanilla ice cream, softened

MAKE IT!

SPOON 1 tsp. syrup into each of 4 glasses. Roll each glass to coat bottom and inside of glass. Finely chop 4 cookies; set aside.

QUARTER remaining cookies; place in blender. Add milk and ice cream; blend until smooth.

POUR into prepared glasses; top with chopped cookies. Serve immediately.

Triple Double **OREO** Tartufo

WHAT YOU NEED!

- 8 Triple Double OREO Cookies, divided
- 1 cup vanilla ice cream
- 1 cup chocolate ice cream
- 3 oz. semi-sweet chocolate
- 1 Tbsp. oil
- 4 maraschino cherries, patted dry

MAKE IT!

CRUSH 4 cookies finely; set aside. Scoop each flavor ice cream into 4 balls. Press 1 whole cookie halfway into center of each vanilla ice cream ball; top with chocolate ice cream ball, pressing together slightly to secure. Roll in cookie crumbs. Place on waxed paper-covered baking sheet. Freeze 2 hours or until firm.

MICROWAVE chocolate and oil in small microwaveable bowl on HIGH 45 sec.; stir until chocolate is completely melted. Cool slightly.

PLACE wire racks over large sheets of waxed paper; top with ice cream balls. Spoon melted chocolate over ice cream balls, using about 1 Tbsp. for each. Top with cherry. Freeze 1 hour or until chocolate coating is firm.

SHORTCUT: Substitute ⅓ cup chocolate-flavored hard-shell ice cream topping for the melted chocolate glaze.

Chocolate-Covered
OREO Cookie Cake

PREP: 20 MIN. | MAKES: 16 SERVINGS.

WHAT YOU NEED!

1 pkg. (2-layer size) devil's food chocolate cake mix

4 oz. semi-sweet chocolate

¼ cup butter

1 pkg. (8 oz.) cream cheese, softened

½ cup sugar

2 cups thawed frozen whipped topping

12 OREO Cookies, coarsely crushed

MAKE IT!

HEAT oven to 350°F.

PREPARE cake batter and bake in 2 (9-inch) round pans as directed on package. Cool cakes in pans 10 min. Invert cakes onto wire racks; gently remove pans. Cool cakes completely.

MICROWAVE chocolate and butter in small microwaveable bowl on HIGH 2 min. or until butter is melted. Stir until chocolate is completely melted. Cool 5 min.

MEANWHILE, beat cream cheese and sugar in large bowl with mixer until blended. Gently stir in whipped topping and crushed cookies. Stack cake layers on plate, spreading cream cheese mixture between layers. Spread top with chocolate glaze; let stand until firm. Keep refrigerated.

FAMILY FUN: This great-tasting cake looks like a giant **OREO** Cookie.

Easy **OREO** Truffles

PREP: 30 MIN. PLUS REFRIGERATING | MAKES: 3½ DOZEN OR 42 SERVINGS, 1 TRUFFLE EACH.

WHAT YOU NEED!

1 pkg. (15.5 oz.) OREO Cookies, finely crushed, divided
1 pkg. (8 oz.) cream cheese, softened
16 oz. semi-sweet chocolate, melted

MAKE IT!

MIX 3 cups of the cookie crumbs and the cream cheese until well blended. Shape into 42 (1-inch) balls.

DIP balls in melted chocolate; place on waxed paper-covered baking sheet. (Any leftover melted chocolate can be stored in tightly covered container at room temperature and saved for another use.) Sprinkle with remaining cookie crumbs.

REFRIGERATE 1 hour or until firm. Store any leftover truffles in tightly covered container in refrigerator.

JAZZ IT UP: Sprinkle truffles with colored sugar or sprinkles in addition to or in place of the cookie crumbs.

Striped Delight

PREP: 20 MIN. PLUS REFRIGERATING | MAKES: 24 SERVINGS.

WHAT YOU NEED!

35 OREO Cookies

6 Tbsp. butter, melted

1 pkg. (8 oz.) cream cheese, softened

¼ cup sugar

2 Tbsp. cold milk

1 tub (12 oz.) frozen whipped topping, thawed, divided

2 pkg. (3.9 oz. each) chocolate instant pudding

3¼ cups cold milk

MAKE IT!

PROCESS cookies in food processor until fine crumbs form. Transfer to medium bowl; mix in butter. Press onto bottom of 13×9-inch dish. Refrigerate until ready to use.

WHISK cream cheese, sugar and 2 Tbsp. milk in medium bowl until blended. Stir in 1¼ cups whipped topping; spread over crust.

BEAT dry pudding mixes and 3¼ cups milk with whisk 2 min.; pour over cream cheese layer. Let stand 5 min. or until thickened; cover with remaining whipped topping. Refrigerate 4 hours.

SPECIAL EXTRA: Drizzle each plate with melted semi-sweet chocolate before topping with dessert square. Sprinkle with crushed candy canes or additional crushed **OREO** Cookies.

Double-Decker **OREO** Cheesecake

PREP: 25 MIN. PLUS BAKING AND REFRIGERATING | MAKES: 16 SERVINGS.

WHAT YOU NEED!

48 OREO Chocolate Creme Cookies, divided

¼ cup butter, melted

4 pkg. (8 oz. each) cream cheese, softened

1 cup sugar

1 tsp. vanilla

1 cup sour cream

4 eggs

4 oz. semi-sweet chocolate, melted

MAKE IT!

HEAT oven to 325°F.

PROCESS 30 cookies in food processor until finely ground. Add butter; mix well. Press onto bottom of 13×9-inch baking pan.

BEAT cream cheese, sugar and vanilla in large bowl with mixer until well blended. Add sour cream; mix well. Add eggs, 1 at a time, beating after each just until blended; pour half over crust. Stir melted chocolate into remaining batter; pour over batter in pan. Chop remaining cookies; sprinkle over batter.

BAKE 45 min. or until center is almost set. Cool completely. Refrigerate 4 hours.

MAKE AHEAD: Wrap cooled cheesecake tightly in foil. Freeze up to 2 months. Thaw in refrigerator overnight before serving.

Chocolate-Caramel Creme Pie

PREP: 30 MIN. PLUS REFRIGERATING | MAKES: 8 SERVINGS.

WHAT YOU NEED!

- 4 oz. (½ of 8-oz. pkg.) cream cheese, softened
- 2 Tbsp. caramel ice cream topping
- 1 cup thawed frozen whipped topping
- 1 OREO Pie Crust (recipe follows)
- 1 pkg. (3.9 oz.) chocolate instant pudding
- 1½ cups cold milk

MAKE IT!

MIX cream cheese and caramel topping in medium bowl until well blended. Gently stir in whipped topping; spread onto bottom of **OREO** Pie Crust.

BEAT dry pudding mix and milk with whisk 2 min.; pour over cream cheese layer. Refrigerate 3 hours.

OREO Pie Crust

PREP: 15 MIN. | MAKES: 1 (9-INCH) CRUST.

WHAT YOU NEED!

- 18 OREO Cookies, crushed (about 1½ cups)
- 3 Tbsp. butter or margarine, melted

MAKE IT!

PLACE cookies in large resealable plastic bag; press bag to remove excess air, then seal bag. Use rolling pin to crush cookies to form fine crumbs.

ADD butter; squeeze bag to evenly moisten crumbs.

PRESS crumb mixture onto bottom and up side of 9-inch pie plate sprayed with cooking spray. Refrigerate until ready to fill.

OREO Chocolate Cheesecake

PREP: 30 MIN. PLUS BAKING AND REFRIGERATING | MAKES: 14 SERVINGS, 1 SLICE EACH.

WHAT YOU NEED!

38 OREO Cookies, divided

5 Tbsp. butter or margarine, melted

5 oz. semi-sweet chocolate, divided

1 pkg. (8 oz.) cream cheese, softened

½ cup sugar

1½ cups sour cream, divided

2 eggs

1 tsp. vanilla

2 Tbsp. sugar

MAKE IT!

HEAT oven to 325°F, if using a silver 9-inch springform pan (or to 300°F if using a dark nonstick 9-inch springform pan).

FINELY crush 24 cookies; mix with butter. Press firmly onto bottom of pan. Stand remaining 14 cookies around inside edge of pan, firmly pressing bottom edge of each cookie into crust. Set aside.

MELT 4 oz. chocolate in small saucepan on low heat; set aside. Beat cream cheese and ½ cup sugar in large bowl with electric mixer on medium speed until well blended. Add ½ cup sour cream, eggs and vanilla; beat until well blended. Add melted chocolate; mix well. Pour over crust.

BAKE 35 to 40 min. or until top of cheesecake is slightly puffed and center is almost set. Mix remaining 1 cup sour cream and the 2 Tbsp. sugar; spread over cheesecake. Bake an additional 5 min. Run knife or metal spatula around rim of pan to loosen cake; cool before removing rim.

MELT remaining chocolate; drizzle over cheesecake. Refrigerate 4 hours. Store any leftover dessert in refrigerator.

NOTE: Garnish with fresh raspberries, chocolate curls and fresh mint just before serving.

OREO Cookie Bread Pudding

PREP: 15 MIN. PLUS BAKING | MAKES: 14 SERVINGS, ABOUT ½ CUP EACH.

WHAT YOU NEED!

4 cups day-old French
    bread cubes (1 inch)

16 OREO Cookies, quartered

2 eggs

2 cups milk

½ cup sugar

¼ cup butter or margarine,
    melted

1 tsp. vanilla

MAKE IT!

HEAT oven to 350°F.

COMBINE bread cubes and cookies in large bowl.

WHISK remaining ingredients until well blended. Add to bread mixture; toss to evenly coat. Pour into 1½-qt. casserole sprayed with cooking spray.

BAKE 45 to 50 min. or until center is set. Serve warm or at room temperature.

OREO Biscotti

PREP: 30 MIN. PLUS BAKING AND REFRIGERATING | MAKES: 28 SERVINGS, 1 BISCOTTI EACH.

WHAT YOU NEED!

18 OREO Cookies, divided

1 cup sugar

⅓ cup butter or margarine, melted

3 eggs

2 tsp. vanilla

3 cups flour

1½ tsp. baking powder

¼ tsp. salt

6 oz. white chocolate, melted

MAKE IT!

HEAT oven to 350°F.

CHOP 2 cookies finely; coarsely chop remaining cookies. Mix sugar, butter, eggs and vanilla in large bowl until well blended. Add flour, baking powder and salt; mix well. Stir in coarsely chopped cookies. Divide dough in half. Use floured hands to shape each half into 8×3-inch loaf on baking sheet sprayed with cooking spray.

BAKE 25 to 30 min. or until golden brown. Cool 10 min. Cut each loaf diagonally into 14 (½-inch-thick) slices. Stand slices on same baking sheet; bake 10 to 12 min. or until lightly toasted. Remove to wire racks; cool completely.

DIP 1 end of each biscotti in melted chocolate. Sprinkle chocolate with finely chopped cookies. Refrigerate until chocolate is firm.

OREO Cupcakes

WHAT YOU NEED!

24 OREO Cookies

1 pkg. (2-layer size) chocolate cake mix

2 cups thawed frozen whipped topping

MAKE IT!

PLACE 1 cookie in each of 24 paper-lined muffin cups. Prepare cake batter as directed on package; spoon over cookies. Bake cupcakes as directed on package. Cool in pans 5 min.; remove to wire racks. Cool completely.

REMOVE paper liners; cut cupcakes horizontally in half.

FILL with whipped topping. Serve cookie-sides up.

NOTE:

These cupcakes are served upside-down so the cookies show on top. If the cupcake tops are rounded, trim off the tops before using to assemble desserts as directed.